Drawing of E. C. Bentley in 1915 by H. G. Riviere
National Portrait Gallery, London

THE FIRST CLERIHEWS

E. CLERIHEW BENTLEY

WITH

G. K. CHESTERTON

L. R. F. OLDERSHAW

EDWARD CHESTERTON

W. P. H. d'AVIGDOR

MAURICE SOLOMON

ILLUSTRATED BY

G. K. CHESTERTON

Oxford New York

OXFORD UNIVERSITY PRESS

1982

Oxford University Press, Walton Street, Oxford OX2 6DP

London Glasgow New York Toronto
Delhi Bombay Calcutta Madras Karachi
Kuala Lumpur Singapore Hong Kong Tokyo
Nairobi Dar es Salaam Cape Town
Melbourne Auckland

and associate companies in
Beirut Berlin Ibadan Mexico City

British Library Cataloguing in Publication Data

Bentley, E. Clerihew
The first clerihews.
1. English wit and humour
I. Title
828'.91209 PN6175

ISBN 0-19-212980-5

Library of Congress Cataloging in Publication Data

Bentley, E. C. (Edmund Clerihew), 1875–1956.
The first clerihews.

Includes a facsim. reproduction of a ms. notebook, entitled 'Dictionary of biography' (54 p.), compiled by Bentley and his friends at St. Paul's School, London, and now in the school's library.
Includes index.
1. Biography – Poetry. 2. Humorous poetry, English. 3. Bentley, E. C. (Edmund Clerihew), 1875–1956 – Manuscripts – Facsimiles. I. Chesterton, G. K. (Gilbert Keith), 1874–1976.
II. Title.
PR6003.E7247F5 1982 821'.912 81-18731

ISBN 0-19-212980-5 AACR2

Printed in Great Britain
at the University Press, Oxford
by Eric Buckley
Printer to the University

CONTENTS

ILLUSTRATIONS

PUBLISHER'S FOREWORD

In October 1981 Oxford University Press published *The Complete Clerihews of E. Clerihew Bentley*, the first collection of all the 140 clerihews published by Bentley in *Biography for Beginners* (1905), *More Biography* (1929) and *Baseless Biography* (1939). (Strangely, the so-called *Clerihews Complete* (1951) in fact lacked thirty-three[1] specimens.) To mark this event, Godfrey Smith ran a competition in the *Sunday Times* for the writing of new clerihews. The announcement of the competition was seen by the Revd A. H. Mead, Librarian of St Paul's School, London, which Bentley had attended at the end of the last century. He wrote to the Press that there was in St Paul's Library a notebook containing clerihews by Bentley and his friends, with illustrations by Chesterton. He thought that perhaps not all of the clerihews had been published, and that we might like to see it.

The notebook turned out to be a far richer source of clerihews than might have been expected. Of the 132 clerihews it contains only twenty-one had been published, and six of these had been significantly altered (a further eleven shared subjects, and sometimes obvious rhymes, with published clerihews, but were otherwise unrelated). The great majority of the clerihews were by Bentley (sometimes in collaboration with his friends), including ninety of the unpublished ones. The standard was variable – after all, the authors were teenagers – but a number of the verses seemed to me as good as any previously known; and Chesteron's illustrations were astonishingly inventive, lively and varied, despite being crammed into the narrow margins of the small book.

[1] Thirty-four if we include a clerihew on Julius Caesar published in *Punch* in 1938, but not reprinted in *Baseless Biography*.

Bentley had evidently not had the notebook before him when he compiled his published books of clerihews. This is clear from his autobiography (see page xvi below), and also from the notebook itself: had he been using it as a source, he would surely have made use of several of the better unpublished verses; he would also have been reminded that some of the clerihews he did include from memory were not in fact his own, but were composed by, or in collaboration with, his friends. But he had given the book to Maurice Solomon in 1893, and it remained in Solomon's possession until his death in 1954, when his widow gave it to St Paul's. (Bentley died two years later.)

It was immediately clear that the notebook ought to be published in facsimile. Thanks are due to Hugh Mead for making this possible by lending the book for reproduction, as well as for providing the note that follows about the St Paul's background, and material for footnotes on St Paul's characters mentioned in the clerihews themselves. Gavin Ewart, John Gilmour, Richard Hardy, Lady Wilkinson and Pat Utechin have also given valuable assistance. Father Antrobus (page 48) was identified by the Very Reverend Charles Dilke, Provost of the Brompton Oratory. Information about Bentley's collaborators and their heirs proved very elusive: Mrs E. M. Denton, Archivist of St Paul's School, provided an indispensable basis for further investigations, and additional data came from D. J. Button, J. H. Chaplin, Councillor Arthur L. Jacob, Basil L. Oldershaw, Peter Oldershaw (who also provided the illustrations on pages xi, xiii and xxiii), R. C. Solomon and Dr R. M. Solomon.

HENRY HARDY

Oxford University Press
1981

BENTLEY AND ST PAUL'S

HUGH MEAD

When Edmund Clerihew Bentley came to St Paul's School in 1887, at the age of twelve, the School had been in its new buildings in the Hammersmith Road for three years. These buildings, designed by Waterhouse, were of red brick, much pinnacled, and could be admired until the 1970s, when they were pulled down by the GLC. There had been about 220 boys when the School moved, but the numbers were rapidly growing. Not long after Bentley left, in 1894, there were 600. Most of them were day-boys. The fees were much lower than at most other famous public schools, and the boys came from all sections of the London middle classes.

'I fear there is something incurably conscientious and solemn about the nature of Paulines', G. K. Chesterton once wrote.[1] Solemnity, at any rate, was not an obvious quality either in him or in Bentley; but conscientiousness was certainly emphasised by the High Master[2] of their day, Frederick William Walker. Every public school, perhaps, has its nineteenth-century GOM, or 'second founder', and such titans are generally well shrouded in myth, nostalgia and anecdote. Bentley and Chesterton were early contributors to the Walker apocrypha, inventing a mechanical master, a malign robot 'supressible only by Walker himself', with his 'reverberating roar of "We don't want yer here!" – terrible words actually uttered by him in extreme cases'.[3] The Walker of a few years later is evoked in Compton Mackenzie's

[1] R. B. Gardiner and John Lupton (eds), *Res Paulinae* (St Paul's School, 1911), p. 242.

[2] i.e. Head Master.

[3] E. C. Bentley, *Those Days* (London, 1940), p. 62.

novel *Sinister Street* and Ernest Raymond's *Mr Olim*. Ernest Shepard sketches Walker (in both senses) in his autobiography *Drawn from Life*.

The historical Walker may or may not be a boojum. But in an introduction to biographical essays of Bentley's kind, one can afford to be rash. Bentley himself calls him 'burly, bearded, red-faced and angry-looking'. A Rugbeian, Walker may have had more in common with Thomas Arnold than some of Arnold's admirers and imitators (though he was a much more colourful man than Arnold, and not so humourless). He despised or ignored many of the idols of the other public schools of his time. He appeared hostile, or at least indifferent, to games, had no prefects except the Captain of the School, crushingly despised social pretension, and had no high opinion of the moral value of boarding. (None the less all these things existed – and some grew – at St Paul's in his day, except prefects, who came soon after it.) What Walker did believe in was intellectual work, and especially a relentlessly thorough linguistic classical grounding; and this he imposed with great success. He believed in it as moral education, but also urged its earthier advantages: 'my boy, you are making a great mistake. If you go in for science, your future is quite uncertain. If you stick to your classics properly, I will undertake to say that you will pay for your education in scholarships and be able to earn £400 a year within a reasonable time afterwards.'[1]

However, this did not prevent Walker allowing, if not encouraging, the growth of other studies at St Paul's. An earlier High Master had firmly told a parent that nothing was taught at St Paul's except Latin and Greek.[2] Walker thought that Latin and Greek were best, and probably thought a classical scholarship at Balliol or Trinity the only proper goal of an intelligent boy; but as soon as possible after his appointment he created a 'Modern Side', gave G. K. Chesterton eighth-form status,[3] despite his refusal to work conventionally, and, in 1893, allowed the formation of the History Eighth, the original members of which included Bentley, Lucian Oldershaw and Edward Thomas, who kept 'a rat or so, and a few snakes' in his desk.[4]

[1] See M. Coutts-Trotter, 'Frederick William Walker', in *Res Paulinae*, p. 124.

[2] 'Madam, at St Paul's we teach only Latin and Greek. We give three half holidays a week that boys may learn mathematics.' Dr Sleath, quoted by F. P. Armitage in *Res Paulinae*, p. 199.

[3] At St Paul's the senior forms are called eighth forms instead of sixth forms.

[4] *Those Days*, p. 58.

The Junior Debating Club, *c*.1890, Oldershaw seated left, G.K.C. centre, Lawrence Solomon immediately behind him, Lawrence's brother Maurice standing extreme right. The others may be d'Avigdor, E. W. Fordham and R. E. Vernede (but possibly Fred Salter is one of them).

The Form Master of the History Eighth, and also Bentley's Housemaster, was R. F. Cholmeley, the subject of the clerihew on page 8, whom Bentley calls 'the most admirable of masters', and whose broad horizons and fairly light-hearted teaching – though he was as intellectually demanding as the High Master himself – may point to 1893, the date of the notebook, rather than 1891, as Bentley's own memoirs imply,[1] as the year of the clerihew's birth. On the other hand 1890 saw the beginning and 1893 the end of a society which involved all five boys who contributed to that birth, the Junior Debating Club. This was a precocious, but far from precious, weekly gathering of boys not yet in the eighth and therefore ineligible for the School's rather ponderous senior debating society, the Union, which tried to model itself on the

[1] See page xv below, note 1.

university Union Societies. The JDC was quite unofficial, though Walker gave it the unexpected and startling encouragement of a favourable mention in public. It confined itself to a dozen members who met by rotation at one another's houses in the evenings – never it seems at Bentley's, which suggests that he may have been a boarder. They discussed with some earnestness – but also perhaps with some irony – such questions as whether collaboration in literature is productive of good results, and the merits of Rudyard Kipling as a writer of short stories. (They were much divided about Kipling: Chesterton parodied his earliest, *Plain Tales*, manner quite effectively in 1892.)[1] On other evenings they discussed 'Three Stages of Ethical Poetry in Europe' or the relative poetic merits of Virgil and Horace (Chesterton championed Horace, Bentley Virgil). They also launched a JDC Chess Club, Antiquarian Society and Naturalists' Society.

They were enviably well-read schoolboys, but the JDC certainly does sound 'conscientious and solemn'. 'We would explain to each other the errors of Darwin and Mr Gladstone', Chesterton recalls[2] – and he also recalls, with a shudder, the poems that he wrote and published in these years. They appeared in the JDC's own magazine, the *Debater*, edited and organised by Oldershaw, which achieved eighteen issues, between March 1891 and February 1893.

Chesterton was Chairman of the JDC,[3] and there can be no doubt that he was its heart. Bentley held him in immense affection and admiration: the relevant chapter of his autobiography is called 'At School with G.K.C.'. Bentley himself was Librarian of the Club (the Library was an arrangement by which they borrowed one another's books); Oldershaw was its secretary. Chesterton, Bentley and Oldershaw were considered, by an anonymous writer in the *Debater*, three of the four 'most earnest and well-read members'.[4] The magazine is full of Chesterton's poems and essays. There are poems by Oldershaw too, and by R. E. Vernede, who was to achieve some success afterwards as a poet of the 'Georgian' school. There are no poems by Bentley, and certainly no clerihews.

All the same, the Club's motto, a graceful tribute to another

[1] *Debater*, vol. iii no. 17 (November 1892), p. 78.
[2] *Res Paulinae*, p. 239.
[3] Hence the gavel as his symbol.
[4] *Debater*, vol. ii no. 5 (July 1891), p. 31.

Oldershaw and Chesterton at the Paris Exhibition, 1900.

Pauline poet,[1] was 'Hence Loathed Melancholy'. Chesterton contributed a rather solemn essay on 'Humour in Fiction' to the *Debater*, mainly interesting as early evidence of his lifelong qualified enthusiasm for Dickens. The tone of the *Debater* is not generally frivolous, even though accounts of the meetings now and again allow a hint of clowning and even horseplay amid all the tea and buns and

[1] On whom see page 30 below.

exuberant intensity. Somewhere between these evenings and the more urbane literary seriousness of Cholmeley's class-room, the Pauline muse hiccupped and the clerihew was born. Something of its spirit already breathes in a series of fables published by Bentley in the *Debater*: the first of them[1] also explains Bentley's symbol in this book:

A Fable

A certain Dodo (now, unhappily, extinct) was one day enjoying the transcient [*sic*] exhilaration produced by excessive indulgence in spirituous and malt liquors. In this state he was perceived by a Blue-ribbon Worm, who approached and read the besotted bird a lecture, in the course of which he touched frequently upon the folly of one who puts an enemy into his Mouth to steal away his Brains. 'Well,' rejoined the degraded *Didus Ineptus*, with a drunken leer, 'since you say you are my Friend, I guess that doesn't apply to me.' With this diabolical remark he seized the doomed *Lumbricus Terrestris* in his unwieldy beak, and instantly devoured him.

Moral – (By the Worm) New brews Schweppe clean,
Mineral waters run cheap.
(By the Dodo) Look not upon the Worm when it is dead,
The Worm will not return.

[1] *Debater*, vol. iii no. 13 (March 1892), p. 6. Another of these fables is reprinted in *Those Days*, p. 144.

THE HISTORY OF THE CLERIHEW

E. CLERIHEW BENTLEY

For nine years, starting when he was about sixteen, Bentley kept a diary, in pursuit of his ambition to be a writer. It is to this diary that he refers at the beginning of the following extract from his autobiography, Those Days, *published in 1940. (Footnotes are editorial.)*

In the diary . . . there is no record of the coming into existence of the sort of nonsense verse that was afterwards to be let loose on the public as *Biography for Beginners*. It must have happened, I think, a little before the diary-keeping began; when my friends and I were about sixteen years old.[1] I do remember that the first inspiration of all came to me in the following form:

Sir Humphrey Davy
Detested[2] gravy.
He lived in the odium
Of having discovered sodium.

From internal evidence it would appear that this was when I had, at my own request, been transferred to the 'science side' of the school; for in the original edition of the book, published in 1905 – say, fifteen years later – the page devoted to this verse had at its foot the following note:

[1] The notebook is dated September 1893, when Bentley was eighteen. Has Bentley misremembered the clerihew's date of birth? Was the notebook not compiled – or the dated dedicatory verses not added – until two years later?

[2] 'Was not fond of' in the notebook, page 7.

> This widely-diffused and abundant element was, in a sense, discovered in 1736 by Duhamel, who first recognized it as a distinct substance; but it was first obtained in the metallic state by Davy in 1807.

Such care for historical accuracy did not mark all the biographies as they subsequently appeared; but in many of them its presence can, I hope, be recognized.

I wrote a number of these – Wren, Erasmus, Roosevelt, Clive,[1] and others, at a sitting one evening: and when G.K.C. and others got hold of the idea there came to be a large output among us. Nothing quite so preposterous had occupied our attention before. They were written in a notebook, with sketches by G.K.C. In course of time, however, the joke began to pall, and it was not until I was launched in life and married that I remembered it again, and the notion of making a publishable book of it occurred to me. The school notebook had vanished (it turned up long afterwards in other hands) and I wanted this in any case to be a book of my own; so I put down from memory a number of verses of my own devising,[2] and G.K.C. illustrated them with imaginative and fantastic pictures which showed his extraordinary gift of drawing at its best, as I think.

As far as I remember, *Biography for Beginners* went to two or three firms before it settled down, in 1905, with Messrs Werner Laurie, who are publishing it still. The name of the author[3] appeared on the cover and title-page of the earlier editions as E. Clerihew; a name which, as I explained in the preface to the fourth[4] edition, 'those who happened to be listening / Heard bestowed on me at my christening'. The illustrator's name was given as G. K. Chesterton, already a name of repute since the appearance of that astonishing book, *The Napoleon of Notting Hill*, in the previous year. For some reason never clear to me, one or two reviewers assumed with confidence that G.K.C. and E. Clerihew were one and the same person. This belief spread and lingered: many years later, for instance, Dr Alington, then Headmaster of Eton, showed, in the course of an article about his favourite

[1] None of these appears in the notebook.

[2] Some, in fact, were not (wholly) his own, if the evidence of the notebook is to be believed.

[3] In the first and second editions E. Clerihew is styled editor.

[4] More properly the third.

books, that the truth was still hidden from him. I wrote to him, reflecting mildly on the state of scholarship in the Etonian cloisters, and had from him a reply so charming in its penitence that, when I published *More Biography* not long after, I dedicated it to him 'in token that all is forgiven'. The first paragraph of the letter in which he acknowledged this impertinence on my part included a detail of literary history that is, I think, worth recording.

> I can't tell you [he wrote] how deeply I was moved on seeing the dedication of your noble volume. No such honour has been paid me since Father Knox, then a boy at Eton, dedicated his first, and I think best, volume to me. I ought perhaps to add that his second volume was dedicated to the Virgin Mary.

But this is to anticipate. *Biography for Beginners*, in spite of G.K.C.'s admirable drawings, had never a popular success; but in course of time it seemed to find its way into the hands of connoisseurs of idiocy everywhere. Nothing was more curious than the difference in taste among those who had each a selected favourite biography. Maurice Baring, for example, awarded the palm to Cimabue: F. V. Knox singled out George Hirst: and D. Spring-Rice – as was natural, perhaps, in a bank-director and hon. secretary of the Political Economy Club – considered Ricardo the best.

I never heard who started the practice of referring to this literary form – if that is the word – as a clerihew; but it began early, and the name stuck. Nor do I know how many people have amused themselves by writing, and even publishing, clerihews; they seem to be countless. Long ago there was an admirable series dealing with the Roman Emperors, written, I believe, by the late Charles Scott-Moncrieff, whom I never met. James Elroy Flecker was also fond of the form: his private output included:

> The sad feature
> About Nietzsche
> Was that the creature
> Thought he was a teacher.

(I wish I had thought of that.) Competitions have been held from time to time in the literary weeklies for the writing of the best clerihew.

One of the prizes was won by my old friend E. W. Fordham, who submitted:

> Miss Mae West
> Was one of the best.
> I would rather not
> Say the best what.

Another prize, some time earlier, was awarded to my son, N. C. Bentley, for:

> Mr Cecil B. de Mille,
> Sorely against his will,
> Was persuaded to leave Moses
> Out of the Wars of the Roses.

The adjudicator, I recall, expressed a suspicion that his father had helped him with his homework; but I had done quite enough of that in years gone by.

I have said that there is no actual record of the birth of *Biography for Beginners*. There is, however, a strictly untruthful account of that occurrence. Some years ago Gerald Barry, who was then editing the *Week-end Review*, asked me for an article dealing with this subject. The request was made, as I gathered from his letter, in the hope that something in the nature of light reading would be forthcoming; and so, taking the suggestion in the spirit in which it was offered, I sent him the following contribution to the history of modern letters:[1]

> When I am asked how *Biography for Beginners*, and the historical method which it initiated, came into existence, my memory turns back to an early spring morning in the last century and a schoolboy's study. I was conning, with the aid of a dictionary, the story of those measures which Julius Caesar had found, to his regret, to be unavoidable in dealing with the Usipetes and the Tencteri. By some association of ideas, the process of which I am unable now to recall, there drifted across my mind – like a rosy sunset cloud softening the white majesty of the Himalaya – the valiant figure of Sir Humphrey Davy. The pen was in my

[1] 'Biography for Beginners', *Week-end Review*, vol. 1 (March–June 1930), pp. 193–5 (issue of 19 April).

hand. Musing, I hardly knew what it was tracing on the page. Then, with a start, I saw that I had written:

Sir Humphrey Davy
Detested gravy.
He lived in the odium
Of having discovered sodium.

So it began.

It was not unnatural that this one of the world's towering figures should present itself for the embodiment of my inspiration. The career of Davy had possessed for me, since infancy, an overmastering fascination. His father's foible of lycanthropy, his mother's descent in the direct line from Attila, had touched my imagination. Adolescent myself, it was with wistful interest that I learned how Davy, as a youth, had been indulged in his passionate fondness for cock-fighting, trout-tickling, and brawling in church. When I found that, in his second term at Oxford, he had been gated for cutting off his tutor's ears, my enthusiasm knew no bounds. I marked with keen sympathy the early establishment of that hatred of gravy which was to colour the whole of Davy's life. I devoured the unholy record of his wild doings as a young man in the London of Weymouth, Dashwood and Rigby; of his duel with the Chevalier d'Eon; of his sensational triumph in the pie-eating contest at Tewkesbury; of his donkey-race against Lord March for a stake of a thousand guineas, each riding with his face to the animal's tail, from Arthur's Club to the Blue Boar at Uxbridge. With mounting admiration I read how, turning his back at length upon idle pleasure, he applied himself successively to oneiromancy, sinology and catechetics before chemistry engaged the unabated ardours of his maturity.

Wan with excitement, I pored over the pages in which Davy's dedication of himself to the discovery of sodium was described. I came to have by heart the text of that volcanic maiden speech in the House of Commons – the speech that made even Dundas tremble, and Jenkinson sob like a child – ending with the imperishable words: 'Is life so dear, or peace so sweet, as to be purchased at the price of deprivation of necessary chemical constituents? Forbid it, almighty God! I know not what course others may take, but as for me, give me sodium or give me death.'

Such was Davy. To epitomise a career such as his – or even one much less crowded and dramatic – within the limits of the literary form devised by me is not by any means an easy task. I have shown that it can be done; but how it is done is a question which I have often had to ask myself. All poets will know what I mean – it is the afflatus, the divine impartation, the rapture. But it is not at all difficult to name some of the things to be avoided in the use of this biographical method.

One must not, in the first place, confine oneself merely to what is historic, in the large sense, about the life that is in question. One has to depict the man as he was, not his achievement only. I may cite as an example of failure in this sense a biography which, because of the weakness I mean, has not been included in either of my published volumes.[1]

Frederick the Great
Became King at twenty-eight.
In a fit of amnesia
He invaded Silesia.

In this there is nothing with which the dry-as-dust historiographer could possibly quarrel. The facts are undeniable. Twenty-eight was Frederick's age when he ascended the throne of Prussia; and in invading Silesia he did forget the existence of the Pragmatic Sanction and his own recent pledge to respect the provisions of that instrument. Yet the biography which I have quoted is a fatally defective one. Truthful and reliable – yes; even slavishly so. But where is the human appeal? Where the probing psychological touch? Frederick, after all, was something more than a dynast, a militarist, and a mental case; but in these sapless lines what hint is given us of the riches of that daemonic personality?

I will give another of the throw-outs, as they may be termed, from the same factory:

[1] i.e. *Biography for Beginners* and *More Biography*. It was not included in *Baseless Biography* either.

Louis Quatorze
Had a penchant for wars.
He sent Turenne to the Palatinate
With instructions to flatten it.

Here again is accuracy; here is, perhaps, history as it should be written. But where is the real Louis? This, I say again, is not biography.

What, then, of the opposite extreme, the fault of too little attention to the circumstances of historical moment in the life of the hero? It must, I suppose, be called a fault; but to my own taste, I confess, it is in the class of amiable weaknesses. Without going so far as to say, with Mr Henry Ford, that 'History is bunk', I do consider that the personal element far transcends it in importance when this special literary form is in question. For example, who can deny the excellence of the following biography, the authorship of which I do not know, and which has not, so far as I know, been published?[1]

The Emperor Pertinax
Possessed a certain axe
With which he used to strike
Those whom he did not like.

This is an admirable presentation, not of the Emperor as he played his part on the world's stage, but of the man as he was known to those nearest and most intimate – a spirit by nature impatient, hasty, temperamental if you will; but sincere, direct, honest, in essence lovable.

But though one may dispense, as I think, with history, what one must have above all is truth – sifted, tested, established veracity. Analysing one's material in this spirit, one courts disillusionment; there will be a loss of much that we have treasured in the human story. I remember too well, for instance, my own chagrin when patient research had convinced me that Oliver Cromwell, as he lay dying at Hampton Court,

[1] According to C. D. Broad, it is by F. W. Haskins. See John Gilmour and Nicholas Wall, 'The Clerihew: Its History and Bibliography', *Book Collector*, vol. 29 (1980), p. 26.

never did say to Dr Goodwin, 'Had I but served my God as I have served my King, He would not have given me over in my grey hairs.' How often, again, have we not been told that Cervantes, on hearing that Dr Sacheverell had passed the Beresina, filled his mouth with pebbles and observed, 'I can make twenty dukes, but not one Titian'? For generations we have believed this. We were foully deceived; the thing is a mere invention, as I have shown.

But by such researches, on the other hand, much that we have valued will be established on the rock of eternal verity, as the skyscraper is stepped in the granite of Manhattan. I have proved, for example, that Henry VIII, on first meeting Anne of Cleves, did after one hurried glance sob convulsively, 'Roll up that map.' I have shown it to be true that Charles Peace never smiled again after his execution at Millbank. Nor, in the face of my investigations, can doubt be any longer thrown on the moving story of how Leonardo da Vinci, on seeing a Lord Mayor for the first time, fell on his knees and burst into tears.

Such things are among the delightful compensations of the exacting, laborious, too often sorrowful task of the biographer.

Although it takes me beyond the intended scope of this book, I may record here the rest of the story of this schoolboy enterprise. It was not until 1929 that, moved thereto by the letter from Dr Alington already mentioned, I published *More Biography*, 'with illustrations by G. K. Chesterton, Victor Reinganum, Nicolas Bentley and the Author'. In the advertisements of the book Mr Reinganum and Mr Bentley (my younger son) were highly spoken of in their association with 'the now world-famous G.K.C.'. Those were early days for them; but I thought then, and think still, that some of their best was in the volume. Reinganum's picture of the Venerable Bede playing Juvenile Lead, with the Anglo-Saxon dramatic critics eyeing the perfomance worse than dubiously from the stalls, was one of the most gravity-removing sketches I ever saw. My one and only contribution to the pictures, depicting the death of William Rufus in the manner of the Bayeux Tapestry, led me to a more intimate study of that matchless work (in Hilaire Belloc's edition) than I had given it many years before. The result was merely a servile imitation; but even that

The Junior Debating Club in 1948, at the Great Western Hotel, before the presentation of a bust of G.K.C. to St Paul's School. From left to right: Fred Salter, Oldershaw, two unidentified gentlemen (one is probably E. W. Fordham), Bentley, unidentified.

can be, and very often is, a labour of love.

Speaking of imitations: not long ago it was suggested to me that if imitation clerihews were so popular, there should be some measure of tolerance for another collection from the original factory. I am not sure that it necessarily follows: people have been known to prefer an imitation to the original: there is a large public, I have heard, for a sort of coffee that has had the caffein taken out of it, and another large public who find that they get swifter results from a kind of port that is manufactured in London than from the kind that is shipped from Oporto. Still, N. C. Bentley and I decided to make the experiment, and the fruits of our collaboration as author and artist appeared in *Punch* during 1938.[1] The last few specimens appeared in 1939. wherein my youthful fancy played; for in my twenties I had written a

[1] The last few specimens appeared in 1939.

great deal of light verse for *Punch*, and if I did not remember much about those contributions, at least I could remember with pleasure that they had got past Owen Seaman – not without emendations by the most minutely critical editor I ever had anything to do with.

When the items of *Baseless Biography*[1] were appearing serially in *Punch*, a curious byway of English eccentricity was forced on my attention. One of my quartets referred to what had taken place 'When their lordships asked Bacon / How many bribes had he taken'.[2] This I wrote innocent of all evil intent; nor do I imagine that the editor, E. V. Knox, was at all prepared for what happened. For many years I, like everybody else, had known of the existence of that school of critics who had satisfied themselves that the works generally attributed to William Shakespeare were written in fact by Francis Bacon, and some of whom were, further, convinced that Bacon was the author of virtually everything else of importance that was published in the reign of Queen Elizabeth. But I had never met in the flesh any one who took either the larger or the lesser view of the cunning deception practiced by Bacon upon his contemporaries and their posterity. I knew that Baconians existed, just as I knew that Seventh-Day Adventists existed and Muggletonians existed, and the people existed who will have it that the earth is flat, or at any rate shaped like a bun; but if I had been asked, I should have ventured the guess that the Baconians were not now that strength which in old days moved earth and heaven, the days when the cryptogram-finders were in the news. How wrong I should have been! For some time after those lines appeared in *Punch*, a cataract of letters of more or less abusive protest from Baconians descended daily upon E. V. Knox's head. They came from all parts of the country and from overseas; especially did they come, I gathered, from our seaside resorts and inland spas. Knox was kind enough to send me, for my enlightenment, a selection from the letters earliest received. One protester made the sweeping statement that 'we are not so rich in genius that we can afford to foul our own nest'. Reference to Bacon as the greatest Englishman who had ever lived was common form in the letters. One declared that he 'gave us our language, the Shakespeare plays and the finest philosophy the world has ever known'. It is one of the mysteries of the human heart

[1] Published in 1939.
[2] See also page 15.

that believers in Bacon's authorship of these plays should feel themselves under the necessity of worshipping Bacon; and that worship of Bacon should be felt to involve detestation and contempt for the attainments and character of Shakespeare, about which hardly anything is known. The same people who quote as decisive evidence Ben Jonson's praise of Bacon never make any reference to Ben Jonson's praise of Shakespeare: to them he is an 'unlettered boor' and 'the Stratford clown'; there is real venom in their attacks. In fact, the whole of the Baconian bosh has about it a very perceptible taint of religious mania.

E. V. Knox must, I think, have felt a sardonic pleasure in its manifestations. One of his best things was the page of humble apology to the Baconians which he wrote for *Punch* after the tumult had subsided. It concluded with the plain confession that there is no proof of Bacon having taken bribes. 'We only know that he said he did.'

NOTE ON THE TRANSCRIPTION

The facsimile of the notebook that follows is interleaved with annotated transcriptions of the clerihews. The pictorial symbols used by Chesterton to show the authorship of each verse are translated into the initials printed in the right-hand margin, except that Bentley's initials have been omitted. EC stands for Edward Chesterton, G. K. Chesterton's father. A question mark means that there is no obvious indication of authorship, and an ampersand (&) that the clerihew in question was written in collaboration with Bentley.

Two sorts of infomation are given in the footnotes, which are numbered according to the order of the clerihews on the page. First, the text is provided (so far as it differs) of all the published clerihews that share subjects with those in the notebook. The published volumes are identified by initials, as follows:

BFB	*Biography for Beginners*
MB	*More Biography*
BB	*Baseless Biography*
CC	*Clerihews Complete*

If no variant text follows one of these sets of initials, the published version is (virtually) identical.

Secondly, persons who may be unfamiliar are briefly identified. In the case of figures connected with St Paul's School, these identifications have been provided by Hugh Mead. The publisher will be grateful to hear from readers who can identify any of the following: J. W. Logan, Mr Carson, Mr Hayes-Fisher (page 14); Doctor Parker (page 35); Mr D. Plunket (page 47).

NOTE ON THE NOTEBOOK

MAURICE SOLOMON

This is the original 'Dictionary of Biography'. The verses are in the handwriting of Edmund Clerihew Bentley and the illustrations are by Gilbert Keith Chesterton. Although Bentley was the originator of the form – since known as the 'clerihew' – and is the author of the great majority of the verses in this book, there were some collaborators. Chesterton has indicated the authorship of each verse by the pictorial signatures, the key to which is as follows:

The Dodo	Edmund Clerihew Bentley
The Gavel	Gilbert Keith Chesterton
The Stag's Head	L. R. F. Oldershaw
The Pipe	G.K.C.'s father
The Double Pi	W. P. H. d'Avigdor
666	Maurice Solomon

As will be seen, Bentley gave the book to me (Grey was my nickname) and I rebound it in boards, the original brown paper cover being bound in. This has altered the order of the verses.

The above is a transcription of a typewritten 'Note', signed by Maurice Solomon, pasted on to the inside of the back board of the new binding to which the note refers. The front of the original cover is shown opposite. The facsimile of the notebook reproduces its pages in their present order.

Lucien Robert Frederick Oldershaw (1876–1951) became a journalist; he was President of the Oxford Union in 1898, and simultaneously President of OUDS. Edward Chesterton was head of a well-known firm of auctioneers and estate agents. Waldo Percy Henry d'Avigdor (1877–1947) later worked for the Alliance Assurance Co. Maurice Solomon (1878–1954) qualified as a Member of the Institute of Electrical Engineers and joined the General Electrical Company, eventually becoming a director.

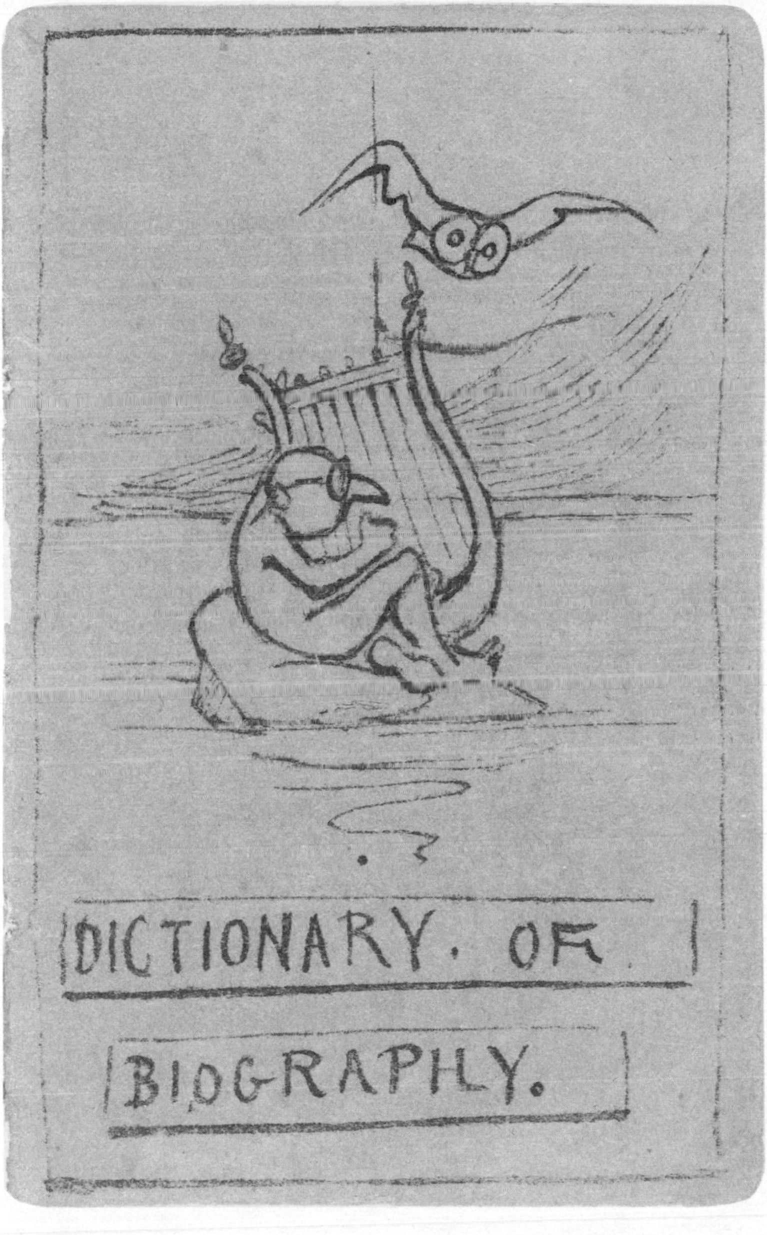
DICTIONARY. OF
BIOGRAPHY.

My Dear Grey:—
Do not throw this away,
Nor consign to the flames
So many illustrious names.

Besides, as I can depone,
Some of the verses are your own.
Therefore treat it the more gently.
Yours sincerely
Edmund C. Bentley.

September 1893.

My Dear Grey :—

Do not throw this away,
Nor consign to the flames
So many illustrious names.

Besides, as I can depone,
Some of the verses are your own.
Therefore treat it the more gently.

Yours sincerely
Edmund C. Bentley.

September 1893.

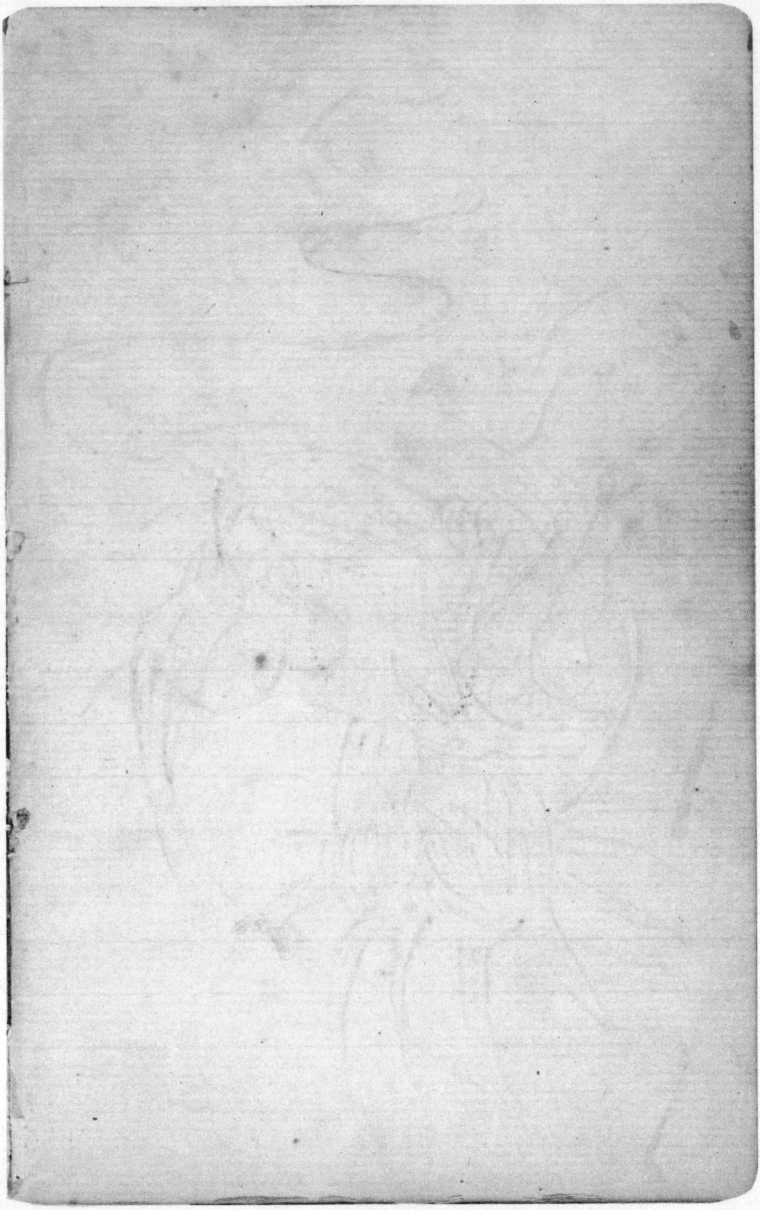

999

Biography

Is different from Geography.
Geography is about maps,
While Biography deals with chaps.

Biography
Is different from Geography.
Geography is about maps,
While Biography deals with chaps.

BFB: The Art of Biography / Is different from Geography. Geography is about Maps, / But Biography is about Chaps.

It is presumably safe to assume that this clerihew (headed 'Introductory Remarks' in BFB) is Bentley's.

Sir Humphrey Davy
Was not fond of gravy
He lived in the odium
Of having discovered sodium.

Mr. W. M. Thackeray
Detested quackery
Among his writings, few comes
Up to the "Newcomes."

1 BFB (Abominated gravy.). In CC 'Detested' replaces 'Abominated'; see also pages xv, xix. 'Humphry' is the usual spelling.

Sir Humphry Davy
Was not fond of gravy
He lived in the odium
Of having discovered Sodium.

Mr. W. M. Thackeray
Detested quackery
Among his writings, few comes
Up to the "Newcomes."

Mr. G. F. Watts
Was not born in Notts
He imposed no strictures
As to the meaning of his pictures.

Christopher Columbus
Proved the earth was not a rhombus.
"Such places," he remarked, "as Berwick are
Not in the least like America."
(666)

Mr. R. F. Cholmeley
Behaved rather rumly.
He thirsted for the serum
Of Jerome K. Jerome.

Mr. G. F. Watts
Was not born in Notts
He imposed no strictures
As to the meaning of his pictures.

Christopher Columbus
Proved the earth was not a rhombus.
"Such places," he remarked, "as Berwick are
Not in the least like America."

MS

Mr. R. F. Cholmeley
Behaved rather rumly.
He thirsted for the serum
Of Jerome K. Jerome.

2 MB: 'I quite realized,' said Columbus, / 'That the Earth was not a rhombus, / But I *am* a little annoyed / To find it an oblate spheroid.'

3 Robert Francis Cholmeley (1862–1948), assistant master at St Paul's School 1886–1909, and afterwards Headmaster of Owen's School, Islington. He was given charge of the history specialist form, when this was created for Bentley and his friends.

John Leech
Had a cheek like a peach.
He couldn't play billiards a bit, but lor!
He *could* draw.

Which was more tall?
Chapman or Hall?
The mystery thickens
When you learn that they published Dickens!
MS

What fools we've been!
We've forgotten the Queen!
She removes her crown, it is said,
When she goes to bed. &MS

1 John Leech (1817–64), artist, cartoonist for *Punch*.
2 BFB: Chapman & Hall / Swore not at all. / Mr. Chapman's yea was yea, / And Mr. Hall's nay was nay.

John Leech
Had a cheek like a peach.
He couldn't play billiards a bit, but lor!
He could draw.

666 Which was more tall?
Chapman or Hall?
The mystery thickens
When you learn that they published Dickens!

What fools we've been!
We've forgotten the Queen!
She removes her crown, it is said,
When she goes to bed.

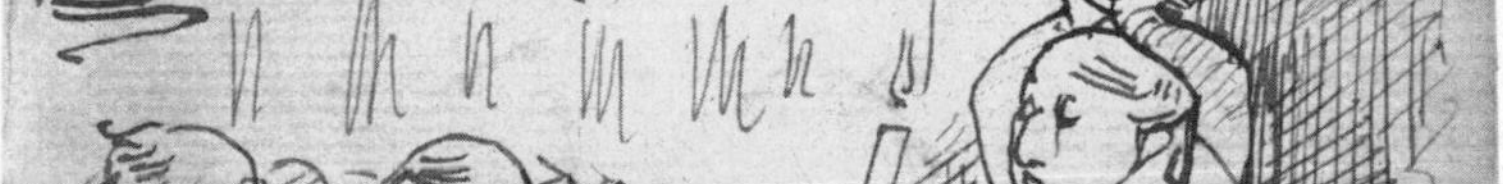

Seeing J. L. Toole
Is better than going to school.
Some think so, at least;
But I consider him a beast.

I expect the friends of Mr. Pemblebury
His body in the sod'll bury.
Though it is his express desire
That it should be thrown in the fire.

666

What a fine book I could concoct on
The works of Frank R. Stockton!
But not half so fine 666
As the one he could concoct on mine.

Seeing J. L. Toole
Is better than going to school.
Some think so, at least,
But I consider him a beast. &MS

I expect the friends of Mr. Pendlebury
His body in the end'll bury.
Though it is his express desire
That it should be thrown in the fire.
&MS

What a fine book I could concoct on
The works of Frank R. Stockton!
But not half so fine
As the one he could concoct on mine.
&MS

1 John Lawrence Toole (1830–1906), comic actor.

2 Charles Pendlebury (1854–1941), mathematics master at St Paul's School, known as 'The Prawn', author of *Pendlebury's Arithmetic.*

3 Frank R. Stockton (1834–1902), American writer of humorous fiction.

James Hogg
Kept a dog,
But, being a shepherd
He did not keep a leopard.

GKC

Philip Massinger
Travelled as a passenger.
It is queer that, in that back age,
He didn't travel as a package.

MS

St. Francis of Assisi
Was all nasty and greasy;
But in spite of that
He wore a halo round his hat.

1 James Hogg (1770–1835), shepherd and poet.
2 Philip Massinger (1583–1640), playwright.

James Hogg
Kept a dog,
But, being a shepherd
He did not keep a leopard.

666 Philip Massinger
Travelled as a passenger.
It is queer that, in that back age,
He didn't travel as a package.

St. Francis of Assisi
Was all nasty and greasy:
But in spite of that
He wore a halo round his hat.

It was bad enough when the Duke of Fife
Left off using a knife,
But people began to talk
When he left off using a fork.

Sir William Vernon Harcourt
Got stouter than a man of mark ought;
But if you come to that
Napoleon was fat.

Guy Fawkes
Has a large box of chalks.
He amused himself with these
In the "Little Ease."

It was bad enough when the Duke of Fife
Left off using a knife,
But people began to talk
When he left off using a fork.

Sir William Vernon Harcourt
Got stouter than a man of mark ought;
But if you come to that
Napoleon was fat.

Guy Fawkes
Had a large box of chalks.
He amused himself with these
In the "Little Ease."

1 BFB (It looked bad when the Duke of Fife).

2 Sir William George Granville Venables Vernon Harcourt (1827–1904), Liberal, Chancellor of the Exchequer 1886 and 1892–3.

Mr. James Bryce
Was not at all nice.
He flew into a temper
And wrote the "Holy Roman Empire."

Mr. John Dillon
Was a blood-thirsty villain.
He demanded why a land
Should be so oppressed as Ireland.

Mr. Robert Browning
Had a horror of drowning.
It is time that you should know it;
He is my favourite poet.

&MS

1 James Bryce (1838–1922), Viscount, Regius Professor of Civil Law at Oxford 1870–93. *The Holy Roman Empire* appeared in 1864.

2 John Dillon (1851–1927), Irish politician, MP for East Mayo 1885–1918.

3 MB: On one occasion when Browning / Saved a débutante from drowning / She inquired faintly what he meant / By that stuff about good news from Ghent.

Mr. James Bryce
Was not at all nice.
He flew into a temper
And wrote the "Holy Roman Empire."

Mr. John Dillon
Was a blood-thirsty villain.
He demanded why a land
Should be so oppressed as Dreland.

Mr. Robert Browning
Had a horror of drowning.
It is time that you should know it;
He is my favourite poet.

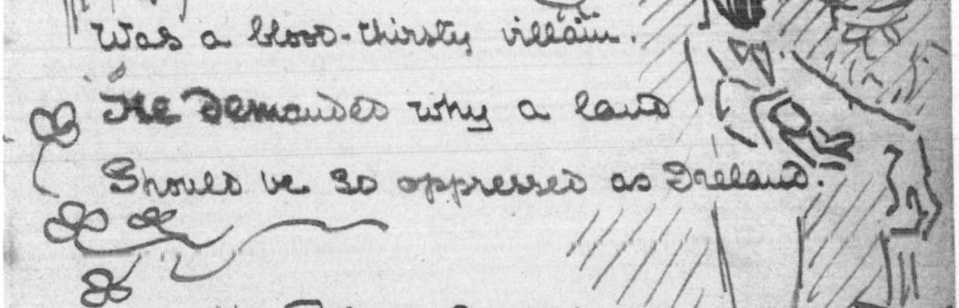

Mr. Charles Dickens
Thought it cruel to kill chickens.
I am sorry for it,
But he wrote "Little Dorrit."

Mr. W. T. Stead
Conversed constantly withe the Dead.
Their joint opinions he would diffuse
In the "Review of Reviews."

Mr. J. W. Rogan
Took a large size of brogan.
He was really the ardent well-wisher
Of Mr. Carson and Mr. Hayes-Fisher.

Mr. Charles Dickens
Thought it cruel to kill chickens.
I am sorry for it,
But he wrote "Little Dorrit." &MS

Mr. W. T. Stead
Conversed constantly with the Dead.
Their joint opinions he would diffuse
In the "Review of Reviews."

Mr. J. W. Logan
Took a large size of brogan.
He was really the ardent well-wisher
Of Mr. Carson and Mr. Hayes-Fisher.

1 MB: It was a pity about Dickens' / Insane jealousy of chickens, / And one could really almost weep / At his morbid distrust of sheep.

2 W. T. Stead (1849–1912), founded *Review of Reviews* 1890, drowned in the *Titanic*.

If you asked bread of Dr. Livingstone
You never found him giving stone.
I wish I had space to describe in this stanza
How he discovered the Victoria Nyanza.

& MS

That objectionable Beau Brummel
Was the kind of man to pummel
I should like to have been there with a red-hot
poker
When he invented the white starched choker.

Sir Francis Bacon
Never had his photograph taken.
How he would roar if he knew how well he
Had been exploited by Ignatius Donnelly!

1 Victoria Nyanza, name given to Lake Victoria by J. H. Speke, who (*pace* ECB and MS) discovered it in 1858.

3 BB: When their lordships asked Bacon / How many bribes he had taken / He had at least the grace / To get very red in the face.

Ignatius Donnelly (1831–1901), American politician and author, leading advocate of Bacon's authorship of Shakespeare's plays.

If you asked bread of Dr. Livingstone

You never found him giving stone. 666

I wish I had space to describe in this stanza

How he discovered the Victoria Nyanza.

That objectionable Beau Brummel

Was the kind of man to pummel

I should like to have been there with a red-hot poker

When he invented the white starched choker.

Sir Francis Bacon

Never had his photograph taken

How he would roar if he knew how well he

Had been exploited by Ignatius Donnelly!

That ass Grant Allen
Wore snow-shoes to walk down Pall Mall in.
I would have my eyes picked out by rooks
Rather than use them to read one of his silly books.

The Rev. J. H. Lupton
Did not care what he supped on.
Praise the Lord for His mercies!
I never did his Latin Verses!

St. Thomas à Becket
Never heard of Reckitt.
The King had recourse to measures drastic
In dealing with that ecclesiastic.

That ass Grant Allen
Wore snow-shoes to walk down Pall Mall in.
I would have my eyes picked out by rooks
Rather than use them to read one of his silly
books.

The Rev. J. H. Lupton
Did not care what he supped on.
Praise the Lord for His mercies!
I never did his Latin Verses.

St. Thomas à Becket
Never heard of Reckitt.
The king had recourse to measures drastic
In dealing with that ecclesiastic.

1 Charles Grant Blairfindie Allen (1848–99), author.

2 The Revd Joseph Hurst Lupton, DD (1836–1905), Fellow of St John's College, Cambridge; Surmaster (= Deputy Headmaster) (1864–99) and Librarian (1876–99) of St Paul's School. Edited Colet's Works.

3 Reckitt, eponym of Reckitt's Blue, a bleach used in laundering.

Dean Colet
Would have hated Smollett.
Whether they ever actually met
I really forget.

&GKC

Samuel Warren
Was more English than foreign.
Reader, shed a tear.
He wrote "Ten Thousand a Year."

LRFO

Cimabue
Didn't know how to cooee.
If you told him he was a Saint
He replied, "I ain't."

1 John Colet (1466?–1519), Dean of St Paul's (Cathedral) and founder of St Paul's School. He intended only Latin and Greek, 'specially Cristyn auctours', to be read there, which perhaps gives point to this clerihew. Cf. 'Erasmus and the Humanists' in BFB: After dinner Erasmus / Told Colet not to be 'blas'mous',/ Which Colet, with some heat, / Requested him to repeat.

2 Samuel Warren (1807–77), lawyer. *Ten Thousand a Year*, his successful novel about Mr Tittlebat Titmouse, appeared in 1839.

3 BFB: When they told Cimabue / He didn't know how to cooee, / He replied, 'Perhaps I mayn't, / But I do know how to paint.'

Giovanni Cimabue (*c.* 1240–1302), Florentine painter.

Dean Colet
Would have hated Smollett,
Whether they ever actually met
I really forget.

Samuel Warren
Was more English than foreign.
Reader, shed a tear.
He wrote "Ten Thousand a Year."

Cimabue
Didn't know how to cook.
If you told him he was a Saint
He replied, "I ain't."

That you have all heard of Hume
I tacitly assume.
But you didn't know, perhaps,
That his parents were Lapps.

I weep over John Bunyan
As though he were an onion.

If I knew a wicked ogress
I would lend her "The Pilgrim's Progress."

Daniel Defoe
Could tie himself in a bow.
He thought it was not
Tying one's legs in a knot.

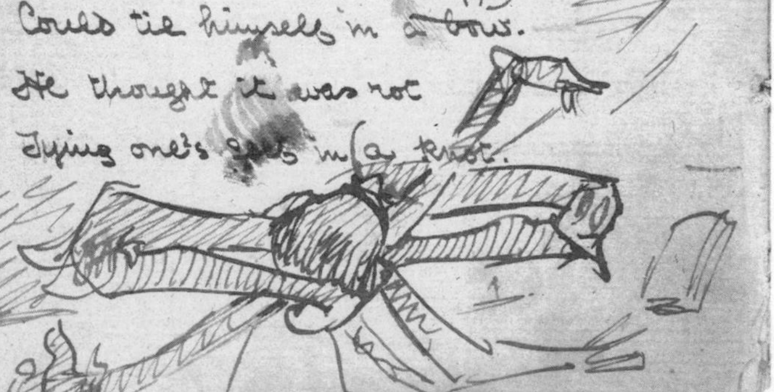

That you have all heard of Hume
I tacitly assume.
But you didn't know, perhaps,
That his parents were Lapps.

I weep over John Bunyan
As though he were an onion.
If I knew a wicked ogress
I would lend her "The Pilgrim's Progress."

Daniel Defoe
Could tie himself in a bow.
He thought it was rot
Tying one's self in a knot.

1 BFB.
2 BFB: I do not extenuate Bunyan's / Intemperate use of onions, / But if *etc.*

Mr. Walter Bésant
Could not touch pheasant.
No doubt I ought to call him Besánt,
But I shan't.

M. *Da*guerre
Etait magnifique, mais n'était pas *la* guerre.
Au maigre homme il rit, grimace horrible au
gras fit,
Et (presque aussi important) découvrit la
photographie.

&MS

We all laugh at Mr. Zangwill;
Even an orang-outang will.
This is strictly *in petto*:
He wrote the "Children of the Ghetto."

1 BFB: Sir (then Mr.) Walter Besant / Would never touch pheasant, / But Mr. James Rice / Thought it so nice.
(Sir) Walter Besant (1836–1901), versatile writer.
3 Israel Zangwill (1864–1926), prominent member of Jewish literary society in England. *Children of the Ghetto* appeared in 1892.

Mr. Walter Besant
Could not touch pheasant.
No doubt I ought to call him Besant.
But I shan't.

M. Daguerre
Était magnifique, mais n'était pas la guerre.
Au maigre homme il rit, grimace horrible au gras fit,
Et (presque aussi important) découvrit la photographie.

We all laugh at Mr. Zangwill;
Even an orang-outang will.
This is strictly in petto:
He wrote the "Children of the Ghetto."

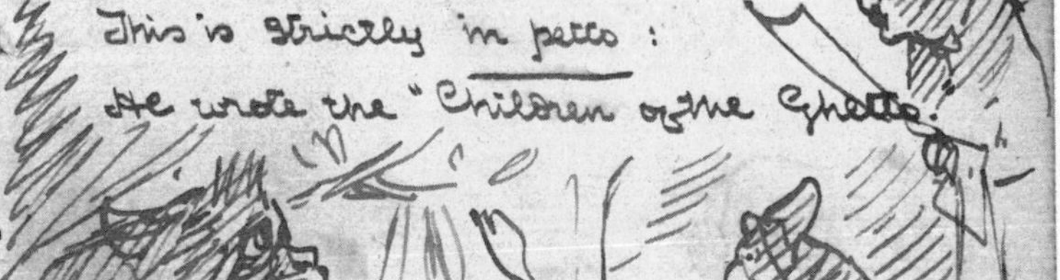

As for Eleonora Duse

I try to pronounce her properly, but it is no use.
She was by no means a failure
In "La Dame aux Camelias."

Mr. Charles Bradlaugh
On his side undoubtedly had law.
Prejudice and bigotry he stamped on
When he took his seat for Northampton.

Mr. Babbage
Lived entirely on cabbage.
He used his head, rather than his thumbs
In inventing his machine for doing sums.

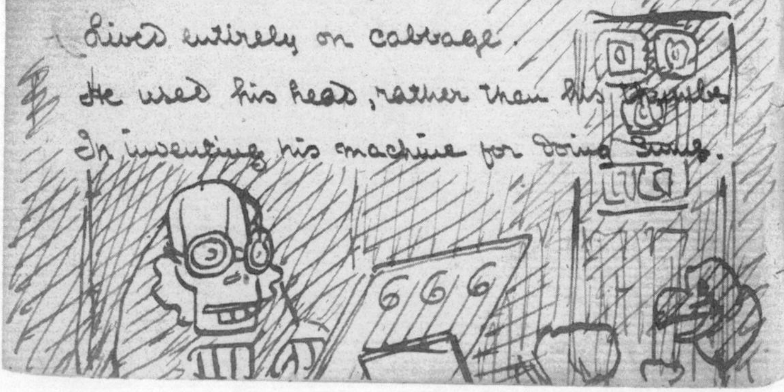

As for Eleonora Duse
I try to pronounce her properly, but it is no
use.
She was by no means a failure
In "La Dame aux Camelias."

Mr. Charles Bradlaugh
On his side undoubtedly had law,
Prejudice and bigotry he stamped on
When he took his seat for Northampton.

Mr. Babbage
Lived entirely on cabbage.
He used his head, rather than his thumbs
In inventing his machine for doing sums.

&MS

1 Eleonora Duse (1859–1924), Italian actress. *La Dame aux camélias* is a social drama by Alexandre Dumas the younger.

2 Charles Bradlaugh (1833–91), proprietor of the *National Reformer*, was elected MP for Northampton in 1880, but refused to swear on the Bible, and was unseated. Re-elected in 1881, he was not allowed to take his seat until 1886.

3 Charles Babbage (1792–1871), inventor of a calculating machine, forerunner of the computer.

Alfred, Baron Tennyson
Deserves our benison.
You can have no conception what a bore I am
When I begin talking about "In Memoriam."

I deny that Mr. John Morley
Has, as so many suppose, a wall-eye.
I don't know that a rationalist
Is so very much worse than a nationalist.

&GKC

Mr. George Merédith
Our modern novelists headeth,
Though some stupid people think a horse
weighs
Less than "Diana of the Crossways."

1 MB: As a young man, Tennyson / Wrote a virelai about venison, / Which falls into the same group / With his sirvente about soup.

2 John Morley (1838–1923), first Viscount Morley of Blackburn, chief secretary for Ireland 1886, 1892–5, prolific author and editor, 'high priest' of rationalism.

Alfred, Baron Tennyson
Deserves our benison.
You can have no conception what a bore I am
When I begin talking about "In Memoriam."

I deny that Mr. John Morley
Has, as so many suppose, a wall-eye.
I don't know that a rationalist
Is so very much worse than a nationalist.

Mr. George Meredith
Our modern novelists headeth,
Though some stupid people think a horse weighs
Less than "Diana of the Crossways."

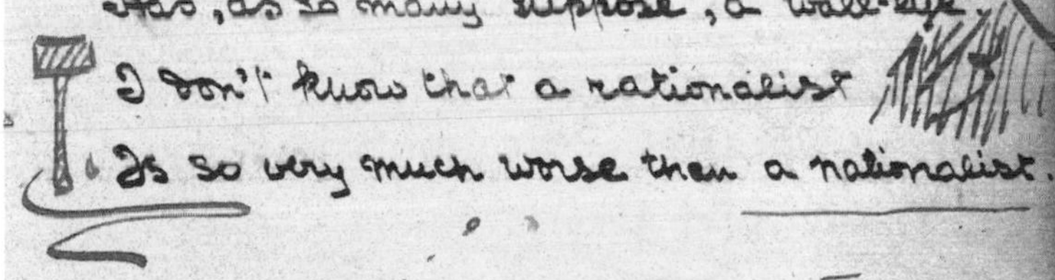

I have heard it said of Thomas De Quincey
That there have been no great prose writers since he.
Than such a statement as that, what could be absurder?
Though the "Opium Eater" is good, and so is the
"Murder."

Mr. Thomas Hardy
Abhorres the Mahdi.
I am bound to confess
I have read worse books than "Tess."

Mr. Henry Fielding
Was most unyielding.
He made no bones
About writing "Tom Jones."

I have heard it said of Thomas de Quincey
That there have been no great prose writers
since he.
Than such a statement as that, what could be
absurder?
Though the "Opium Eater" is good, and so is
the "Murder."

Mr. Thomas Hardy
Abhorred the Mahdi.
I am bound to confess
I have read worse books than "Tess."

Mr. Henry Fielding
Was most unyielding.
He made no bones
About writing "Tom Jones." & WPHd'A

Sir Frederick Abel
Sat on the table;
And I am by no means sure
He didn't sit on the floor.

Louis XI
Was contemporary with Henry VII.
I am very glad he
Was not contemporary with me.

EC, WPHd'A

In reading Robert Burns
What a lot one learns.
He said a king could make a belted knight
And he was right.

&GKC

1 Sir Frederick Augustus Abel (1827–1902), chemist, student of explosives.

2 MB (I am glad that he).

3 BB: 'Gentlemen,' said Burns, / 'Before the meeting adjourns / I think the least we can do / Is to declare that we are nae fou.'

Sir Frederick Abel
Sat on the table;
And I am by no means sure
He didn't sit on the floor.

Louis XI
Was contemporary with Henry VII.
I am very glad he
Was not contemporary with me.

In reading Robert Burns
What a lot one learns.
He said a King could make a belted Knight
And he was right.

Lord Rosebery
In the Foreign Office papers would his nose bury:
But you are not to suppose
That he was ashamed of his nose.
Solomon
You can scarcely write less than a crown on.
His very song
Was long.
The views of Pizarro
Were rather narrow.
He killed the Caciques
Alleging that they were sneaks.

Lord Rosebery
In the Foreign Office papers would his nose
bury:
But you are not to suppose
That he was ashamed of his nose. & GKC

Solomon
You can scarcely write less than a column on.
His very song
Was long. GKC

The views of Pizarro
Were rather narrow.
He killed the Caciques
Alleging that they were sneaks. & EC

1 Arthur Philip Primrose Rosebery (1847–1929), fifth earl of Rosebery, Foreign Secretary in the Gladstone governments of 1886 and 1892 (and Prime Minister in 1894–5).

3 BFB: The views of Pizarro / Were perhaps a little narrow. / He killed the Caciques / Because (he said) they were sneaks.

It was not Napoleon
Who founded the Ashmolean.
He never had the chance,
Living mostly in France.

Let me detain you a moment
To tell you about Beaumont.
He said, "I *will* write a play;"
And he had his way. & MS

G. A. Henty
Has written more books than twenty.
Isn't it sad?
They're all so bad. MS

It was not Napoleon
Who founded the Ashmolean.
He never had the chance,
Living mostly in France.

666

Let me detain you a moment
To tell you about Beaumont.
He said, "I *will* write a play"
And he had his way.

G. A. Henty
Has written more books than twenty.
Isn't it sad?
They're all so bad.

666

When last at Berlin, Mr. Chamberlain
Murmured sadly, "This is not the same Berlin."
I daresay he never was there,
But I don't care.

Of Charles the Great
I do not know the date,
But at any rate
It began with an E.

Fenimore Cooper
Swore like a trooper
He wrote the "Scout"
As far as I can make out.

When last at Berlin, Mr. Chamberlain
Murmured sadly, "This is not the same Berlin."
I daresay he never was there,
But I don't care.

Of Charles the Great
I do not know the date.
But at any rate
It began with an 8.

Fenimore Cooper
Swore like a trooper.
He wrote the "Scout"
As far as I can make out.

3 James Fenimore Cooper (1789–1851), American novelist. He does not appear to have written a book entitled *The Scout*.

If Mr. R. L. Stevenson only spelt his name
Stevensong
He would rhyme accurately to evensong.
He wrote many books, but never wrote a
biography of Noah,
And I wish he wouldn't stay in Samoa.

& MS

Charles Stuart Parnell
Has long been in the charnel.
His name they still revere in
Erin, Green Erin.

& WPHd'A

Dr. Oliver Wendell Holmes,
When irritated, foams.
In the course of a very long life
He has only had one wife.

1 Stevenson lived in Samoa from 1888 until his death in 1894.

3 Oliver Wendell Holmes (1809–94), Professor of Anatomy and Physiology at Harvard 1847–82, essayist.

If Mr. R. L. Stevenson only spelt his name Ste-venson,
He would rhyme accurately to evensong.
He wrote many books, but never wrote a biography of Noah,
666 And I wish he wouldn't stay in Samoa.

III

Charles Stuart Parnell
Has long been in the charnel,
His name they still revere in
Erin, Green Erin.

Dr. Oliver Wendell Holmes,
When irritated, foams.
In the course of a very long life
He has only had one wife.

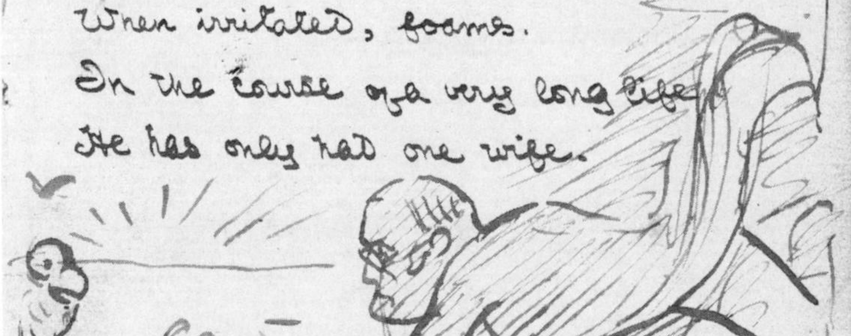

Mr. Samuel Pepys

Eternally sleeps.

On instituting an enquiry

I found he wrote a Diary.

Whenever William Cobbett

Saw a hen-roost, he would rob it.

He posed as a British Farmer,

But knew nothing about Karma.

Edmund Spenser

Could decline "mensa."

He was over sixteen

When he wrote the "Faerie Queene."

Mr. Samuel Pepys
Eternally sleeps.
On instituting an enquiry
I found he wrote a Diary.

Whenever William Cobbett
Saw a hen-roost, he would rob it.
He posed as a British Farmer,
But knew nothing about Karma.

& GKC

Edmund Spenser
Could decline "mensa."
He was over sixteen
When he wrote the "Faerie Queene."

3 MB: How vigilant was Spenser / As a literary censor! / He pointed out that there were too few E's / In Lily's *Euphues*. (This is a reference to John Lyly (1554?–1606), grandson of William Lily, first High Master of St Paul's School – these are the usual spellings.)

Sir Walter Scott
Wrote a lot.
"What is his best book?" is a gigantic query,
But I answer boldly, "The Antiquary."

Richard Brinsley Sheridan
Is now a buried one.
He was not a Goth, much less a Vandal,
As he proved by writing the "School for
Scandal"

Mr. Andrew Lang
Very seldom sang
He criticized Heine
And wrote "Ballades of Blue China."

1 BB: I believe it was admitted by Scott / That some of his novels were rot. / How different was he from Lytton, / Who admired everything he had written! (Lytton is the subject of a clerihew on page 45.)

3 Andrew Lang (1844–1912), writer: his *Ballades in Blue China* (*sic*) appeared in 1880–1.

Sir Walter Scott
Wrote a lot.
"What is his best book?" is a gigantic query,
But I answer boldly, "The Antiquary."

Richard Brinsley Sheridan
Is now a buried one.
He was not a Goth, much less a Vandal,
As he proved by writing the "School for Scandal."

Mr. Andrew Lang
Very seldom sang
He criticized Heine
And wrote "Ballades of Blue China."

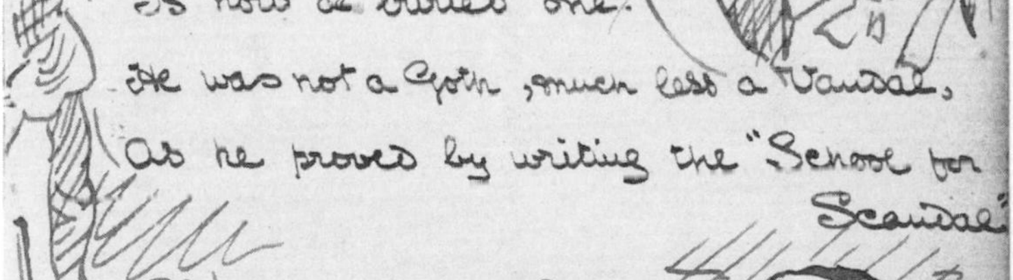

John Milton
Preferred Cheddar to Stilton.
He placed the Devil
On an entirely new level.

President Lincoln
Disapproved of the "Pink 'Un."
The width of his mouth
Was a standing joke in the South.

Saul
Was tall.
David cut off the end of his cloak
For a joke.

John Milton
Preferred Cheddar to Stilton.
He placed the Devil
On an entirely new level.

President Lincoln
Disapproved of the "Pink 'Un."
The width of his mouth
Was a standing joke in the South.

& EC

Saul
Was tall.
David cut off the end of his cloak
For a joke.

& GKC

1 MB: The digestion of Milton / Was unequal to Stilton. / He was only feeling so-so / When he wrote *Il Penseroso*.

2 *The Pink 'Un*, a horse-racing magazine, also containing gossip.

Mr. Grote
Had a funny note
All about his way
Of changing C into K. LRFO

The novels of Jane Austen
Are the ones to get lost in.
I wonder if Labby
Has read "Northanger Abbey."

GKC

Van Eyck
Was christened Jan, not Mike.
This curious mistake
Often kept him awake.

1 George Grote (1794–1871), politician and historian.

2 BFB. 'Labby' is a nickname of Henry Du Pré Labouchere (1831–1912), English journalist and radical.

3 BFB: The younger Van Eyck / Was christened Jan, and not Mike. / The thought of this curious mistake / Often kept him awake.

Mr. Grote
Has a funny note
All about his way
Of changing C into K.
The novels of Jane Austen
Are the ones to get lost in.
I wonder if Labby
Has read "Northanger Abbey."
Van Eyck
Was christened Jan, not Mike!!
This curious mistake
Often kept him awake

Walter Pater
Was not a Satyr,
But he would have liked to be an
Epicurean.

Percy Bysshe Shelley
Wrote a poem about jelly.
It was before he was drowned
That he wrote "Prometheus Unbound."

The Duke of Argyll
Made his speeches from a stile.
He said there was no sense
In making them from the fence.

Walter Pater
Was not a Satyr,
But he would have liked to be an
Epicurean.

& WPHd'A

Percy Bysshe Shelley
Wrote a poem about jelly.
It was before he drowned
That he wrote "Prometheus Unbound."

The Duke of Argyll
Made his speeches from a stile.
He said there was no sense
In making them from the fence.

William Frith
Is not a myth.
This is tiresome, because
I wish he was.

When they christened Laurence Oliphant
He observed, "What a jolly font."
This irreverent remark
Was overheard by the Clerk. & GKC

Mr. William Whitely
Was most unsightly.
He sold nothing but cyder
And called that being a Universal Provider.

GKC, EC

1 William Powell Frith (1819–1909), painter.

2 Laurence Oliphant (1829–88), journalist and traveller.

3 William Whiteley (*sic*) (1831–1907), merchant, creator of the department store.

William Frith
Is not a myth.
This is tiresome, because
I wish he was.

When they christened Lawrence Oliphant
He observes, "What a jolly font."
This irreverent remark
Was overheard by the Clerk.

Mr. William Whitely
Was most unsightly.
He sold nothing but cyder
And called that being a Universal Provider.

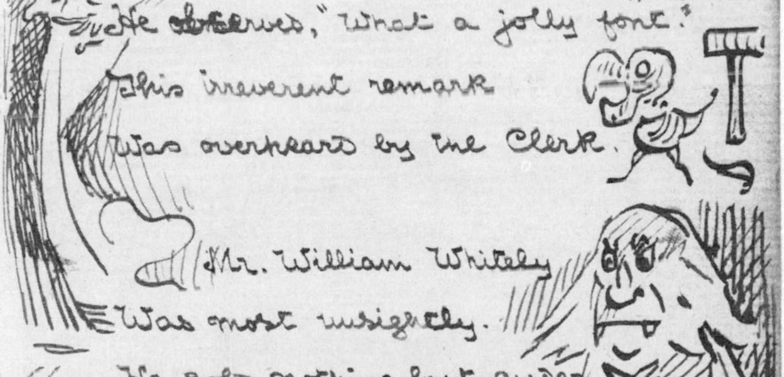

Though Irish, Laurence Sterne
Was no mere kerne
If he has been a kerne, he
Couldn't have written "A Sentimental Journey."

I am not Mahomet;
Far from it.
In the East one constantly is met
With the observation "Kismet."

Sir Richard Steele
Lived on orange peel;
But he kept quite quiet
About this diet.

Though Irish, Lawrence Sterne
Was no mere kerne
If he had been a kerne, he
Couldn't have written "A Sentimental Journey."

& GKC

I am not Mahomet;
Far from it.
In the East one constantly is met
With the observation "Kismet."

Sir Richard Steele
Lived on orange peel;
But he kept quite quiet
About this diet.

& GKC

1 Sterne's first name is usually spelt 'Laurence'.

2 BFB: I am not Mahomet. / – Far from it. / That is the mistake / All of you seem to make.

3 Sir Richard Steele (1672–1729), writer and journalist.

It is a peculiarity of Ruskin
Never to wear a buskin.
I advise you to spend your pennies
On "The Stones of Venice."

& GKC

They say that Cadbury
Never uses a bad berry.
From the Poles to the Orinoco
You hear of nothing but his cocoa.

& MS

Doctor Parker
Was no relation to T'Chaka.
He wrote to the "Times;"
But that was the least of his crimes.

GKC

1 There was no *double entendre* in the third line in 1893. The second sense is not attested before 1945.

3 Doctor Parker's identity is uncertain. T'Chaka (*c.* 1789–1828), often 'Shaka', founder of Zulu empire in Southern Africa.

It is a peculiarity of Ruskin
Never to wear a buskin.
I advise you to spend your pennies
On "The Stones of Venice."

They say that Cadbury
Never uses a bad berry.
From the Poles to the Orinoco
You hear of nothing but his cocoa.

Doctor Parker
Was no relation to T'Chaka.
He wrote to the "Times;"
But that was the least of his crimes.

Joseph Addison
Was a Paddy's son.
It was he, not his pater,
Who edited the "Spectator."

Mr. Henry Irving
Was most unnerving.
He uttered strange yells
In "The Bells."

"Currer Bell"
Was all very well;
I like her rather,
But as for her father——!

Joseph Addison
Was a Paddy's son.
It was he, not his pater,
Who edited the "Spectator."

WPHd'A

Mr Henry Irving
Was most unnerving.
He uttered strange yells
In "The Bells."

& GKC

"Currer Bell"
Was all very well;
I like her rather,
But as for her father —!

GKC, WPHd'A

2 (Sir) Henry Irving (1838–1905), actor, appeared in the melodrama *The Bells* in 1871–2.

Savonarola
Did not wear a bowler.
He said man could not serve God and Mammon
But that was gammon.

& GKC

M. Jules Verne
Ne demeura jamais à Nairn.
Il ne parle pas du Salon
Dans "Cinq Semaines en Ballon."

Mr. Mark Twain
Was better off than Cain.
He got his money
By being funny.

1 MB: Savonarola / Declined to wear a bowler, / Expressing the view that it was gammon / To talk of serving God and Mammon.

Savonarola
Did not wear a bowler.
He said man could not serve God and Mammon
But that was gammon.

M. Jules Verne
Ne demeura jamais à Nairn
Il ne parle pas du Salon
Dans "Cinq Semaines en Balloon."

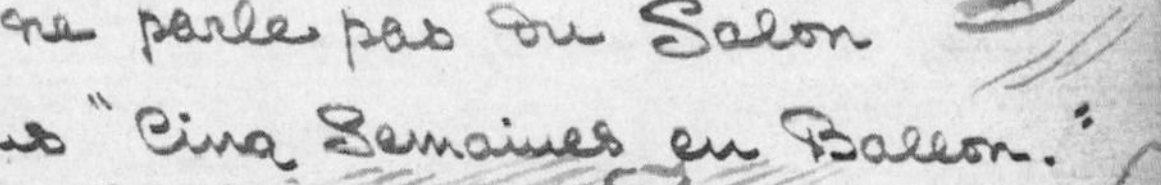

Mr. Mark Twain
Was better off than Cain.
He got his money
By being funny.

Paderewski
Was born under the blue sky.
Unlike Hanno,
He played on the piano.
Mr. G. Austen
Drank coffee, and, when he had the chance, tea.
He considered it risky
To drink nothing but whiskey.
Andrea del Sarto
Called a turnip a tomato.
He attained publicity
Through this eccentricity.

Paderewski
Was born under the blue sky.
Unlike Hanno,
He played on the piano. & GKC

Mr. F. Anstey
Drank coffee, and, when he had the chance, tea.
He considered it risky
To drink nothing but whiskey.

Andrea del Sarto
Called a turnip a tomato.
He attained publicity
Through this eccentricity.

2 F. Anstey, pseudonym of Thomas Anstey Guthrie (1856–1934), novelist, writer for *Punch*.

3 Andrea del Sarto (1486–1530), Florentine painter.

The novels of George Eliot
In thousands sell yet.
Those who do as they're bid'll march
Straight out and buy "Middlemarch."

When the late Titian
Was in a critical condition
He was carefully nursed
By Francis I.

When Mr. J. A. Froude
Saw a cow, he mooed.
We find no mention of the Bermudas
In his history of the Tudors.

2 BFB (When the great Titian). In CC 'late' appears as above.

3 James Anthony Froude (1818–94) became Regius Professor of Modern History at Oxford in 1892.

The novels of George Eliot
In thousands sell yet.
Those who do as they're bid'll march
Straight out and buy "Middlemarch".

When the late Titian
Was in a critical condition
He was carefully nursed
By Francis I.

When Mr. J. A. Froude
Saw a cow, he mooed.
We find no mention of the Bermudas
In his history of the Tudors.

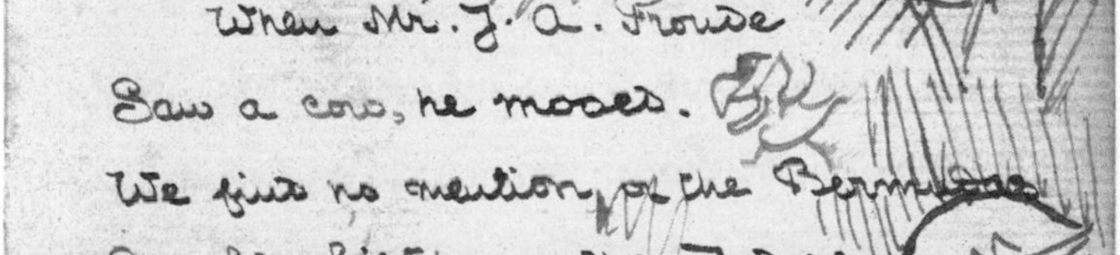

Did not read the Globe.

Nothing could be higher than

His opinion of the Leviathan.

Sir Isaac Newton

Was a thorough Teuton.

Some people will have it he

Discovered gravity.

C'était l'habitude de M. Zola

De crier, sous toutes circonstances, "Hola."

(Here our French fails us.) The perverted old rascal

Vindicates his philosophy in "Le Docteur Pascal."

Job
Did not read the "Globe."
Nothing could be higher than
His opinion of the Leviathan. ?

Sir Isaac Newton
Was a thorough Teuton.
Some people will have it he
Discovered gravity.

C'était l'habitude de M. Zola
De crier, sous toutes circonstances, "Hola."
(Here our French fails us.) The perverted old
rascal
Vindicated his philosophy in "Le Docteur
Pascal."

1 BFB: It is understood that Job / Never read *The Globe*; / But nothing could be higher than / His opinion of Leviathan.

F. C. Burnand
Built his house on the sand.
He edited "Punch"
With an interval for lunch.

It is curious that Handel
Should have used a candle.
Men of his stamp
Generally use a lamp.

The elder Pitt
Had a fit.
He anathematized France
Whenever he got a chance.

1 Francis Cowley Burnand (1836–1917), editor of *Punch* 1880–1906.

2 MB (Should always have used a candle.). Does the dodo between 2 and 3 apply to both?

F. C. Burnand
Built his house on the sand.
He edited "Punch"

With an interrogation hunch.

It is curious that Handel
Should have used a candle.
Men of his stamp
Generally use a lamp.

The elder Pitt

Had a fit.
He anathematized France
Whenever he got a chance.

If we had thrown writings at Herodotus
He would have been perfectly justified in throwing cod at us.
It always has been and will be a mystery
How he could have the impudence to call his writings "History."

Edward Gibbon
Was not "Blue Ribbon."
He died too soon
To read "Lorna Doone."

Wynkyn de Worde
Had as funny a name as ever I heard.
Of what could they have been thinking
When they called him Wynkyn?

If we had thrown whitings at Herodotus
He would have been perfectly justified in
throwing cod at us.
It always has been and will be a mystery
How he could have the impudence to call his
writings "History."

Edward Gibbon
Was not "Blue Ribbon."
He died too soon
To read "Lorna Doone."

Wynkyn de Worde
Had as funny a name as ever I heard.
Of what could they have been thinking
When they called him Wynkyn?

3 Wynkyn de Worde (*fl.* 1477–1535), printer, Caxton's assistant and successor. His real name was Jan van Wynkyn.

Conan Doyle
Ought to be boiled in oil.
He makes no reference to gnomes
In "The Adventures of Sherlock Holmes."

The Spanish people think Cervantes
Equal to half a dozen Dantes;
An opinion resented most bitterly
By the people of Italy. GKC

Edward the Confessor
Slept under the dresser.
When that began to pall
He slept in the hall.

2 BFB. 3 BFB.

Conan Doyle
Ought to be boiled in oil!
He makes no reference to gnomes
In "The Adventures of Sherlock Holmes".

The Spanish people think Cervantes
Equal to half a dozen Dantes:
An opinion resented most bitterly
By the people of Italy.

Edward the Confessor
Slept under the dresser.
When that began to pall
He slept in the hall.

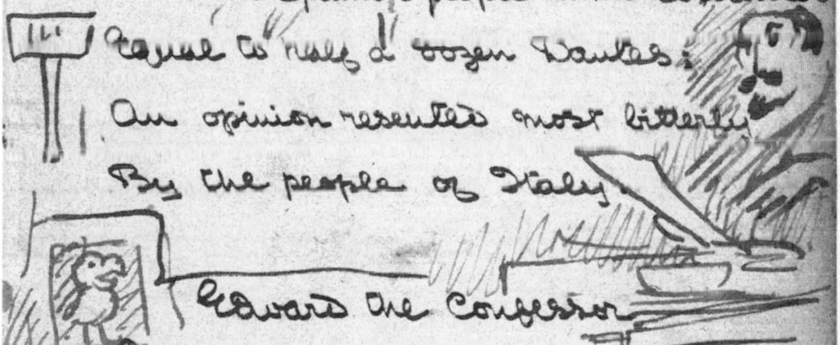

Thomas Carlyle
Has been forgotten all this while.
He wrote "Sartor Resartus,"
But that shan't part us.
Voltairê
Sut faire.
Il ne commencea jamais un livre
Jusqu'à ce qu'il fût tout-à-fait ivre.
To the Irish people said Mr. Gladstone,
"The lands which formarey thou hadst, own."
He never chopped down the thinnest tree
Without thinking how it would affect
his Ministry.

Thomas Carlyle
Has been forgotten all this while.
He wrote "Sartor Resartus,"
But that shan't part us. GKC

Voltaire
Sut faire.
Il ne commencea jamais un livre
Jusqu'à ce qu'il fût tout-à-fait ivre.

To the Irish people said Mr. Gladstone,
"The land which formerly thou hadst, own."
He never chopped down the thinnest tree
Without thinking how it would affect his
Ministry.
?

1 MB (Suffered with his bile.).
2 BB: It was a weakness of Voltaire's / To forget to say his prayers, / And one which to his shame / He never overcame.

Of the prophet Ezekiel
I do not wish to speak ill;
But he himself owns
He saw a Valley of Dry Bones.

& GKC

John Pym
Always said, "Sink or swim,"
But I should think twice
Before taking his advice.

Lord Lytton
I should like to have bitten.
I unhesitatingly assert
That his little soul was dirt.

2 John Pym (1854–1643), parliamentarian.

3 Edward George Earle Lytton Bulwer-Lytton (1803–73), first Baron Lytton, politician and writer. See also page 29, note 1.

Of the prophet Ezekiel
I do not wish to speak ill;
But he himself owns
He saw a Valley of Dry Bones.

John Pym
Always said, "Sink or swim,"
But I should think twice
Before taking his advice.

Lord Lytton
I should like to have bitten.
I unhesitatingly assert
That his little soul was dirt.

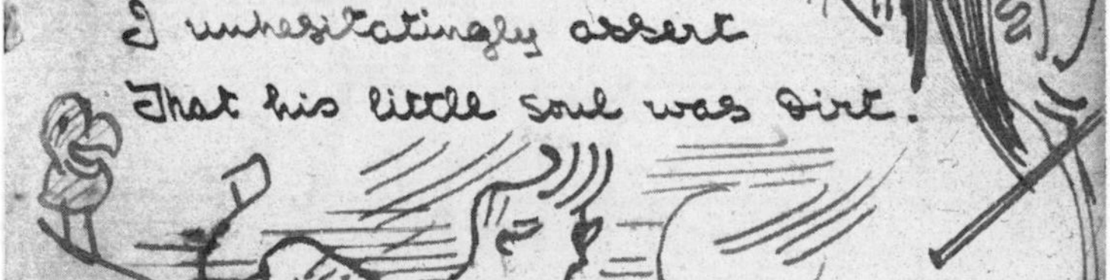

Alexandre Dumas
(Le père) était gras.
Il a l'air
D'avoir écrit "Les Trois Mousquetaires."
J. H. Spurgeon
Was a queer old sturgeon.
His opponents he would tackle
In a tabernacle.
The Abbé Liszt
Hit the piano with his fist.
That was the way
He used to play.

Alexandre Dumas
(Le père) était gras.
Il a l'air
D'avoir écrit "Les Trois Mousquetaires."

J. H. Spurgeon
Was a queer old sturgeon.
His opponents he would tackle
In a tabernacle.
& GKC, EC, WPHd'A

The Abbé Liszt
Hit the piano with his fist.
That was the way
He used to play.
WPHd'A

2 Presumably a mistake for C. H. Spurgeon (1834–92), English baptist preacher of strong convictions. The Metropolitan Tabernacle, Newington Causeway, was built in 1859–61 specially to house Spurgeon's huge audiences.

3 BFB.

Michael Angelo
Thought sand yellow,
And it is not for me
To disagree.

John Stuart Mill
Is cold and still.
I have always understood
That his Principles were good.

Whenever Mr. D. Plunket
Saw a bottle of wine, he drunk it.
His heart was observed to be bleeding
On the night of the Third Reading.

2 BFB: John Stuart Mill, / By a mighty effort of will, / Overcame his natural bonhomie / And wrote *Principles of Political Economy*.

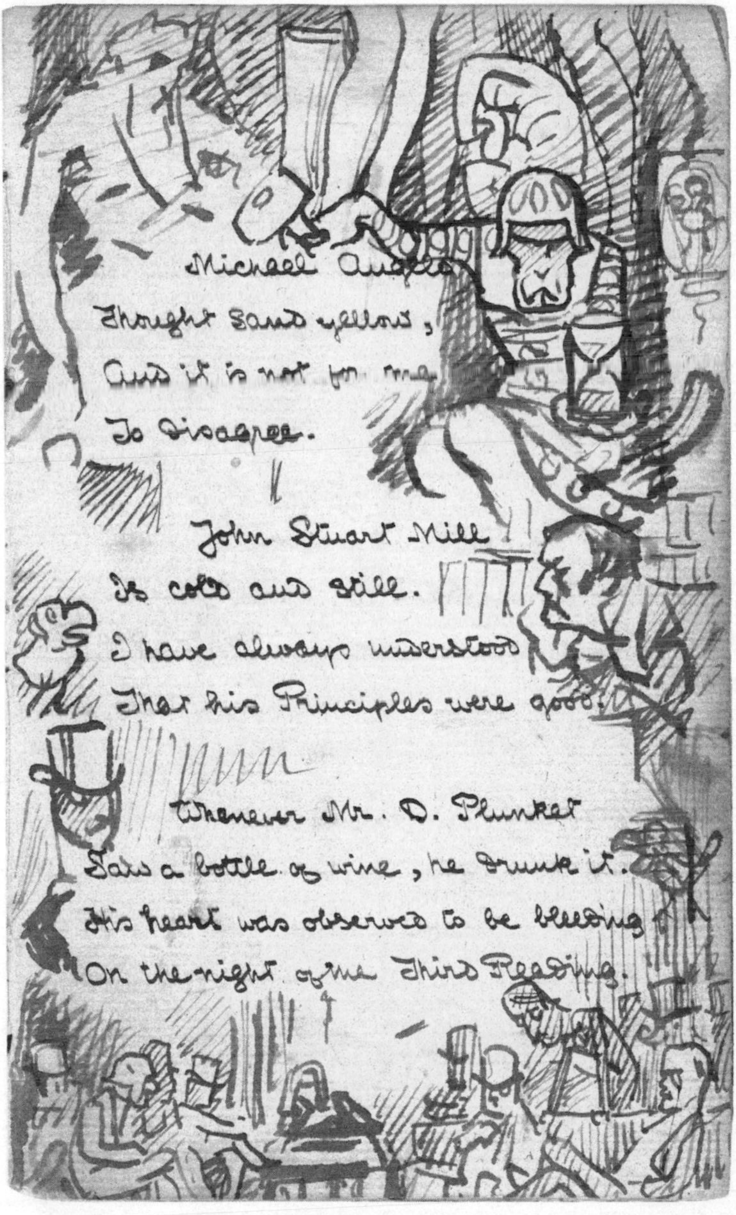
Michael Angelo
Thought sand yellow,
And it is not for me
To disagree.
John Stuart Mill
Is cold and still.
I have always understood
That his Principles were good.
Whenever Mr. D. Plunket
Saw a bottle of wine, he drunk it.
His heart was observed to be bleeding
On the night of the Third Reading.

It really mattered little to Oliver Cromwell
Whether his water was from river or from well
He actually had the face
To order the removal of the mace.

Mr. T.P. O'Connor
Was the soul of honour.
But the conceit of that young Irish
Was something of the infernalest.

Dear old Father Antrobus!
We're Protestants, so he can't rob us.
He doesn't care twopence for a Whig or for a Tory.
And is the life and soul of the Brompton Oratory.

It really mattered little to Oliver Cromwell
Whether his water was from river or from well
He actually had the face
To order the removal of the mace.

Mr. T. P. O'Connor
Was the soul of honour.
But the conceit of that journalist
Was something of the infernalest.

Dear old Father Antrobus!
We're Protestants, so he can't rob us.
He doesn't care twopence for a Whig or for a
Tory,
And is the life and soul of the Brompton
Oratory.

2 T. P. O'Connor (1848–1929), journalist and author.

3 Father Antrobus (1837–1903), diplomat in early life, convert to Roman Catholicism, priest of the Oratory from 1869, translated works of Church history.

Mr. Oscar Wilde
Got extremely riled.
He ejaculated, "Blow me
If I don't write 'Salomé.'"

Jean-Jacques Rousseau
N'était pas Garde *du* Sceau.
Ni moi non plus.
Et vous?

When they asked Mr. Edison
What relation he was to his father, he said,
"His son:"
A curious position
For so prominent an electrician. & MS

2 *Garde des Sceaux* (*sic*) ('Keeper of the Seals'), title of France's minister of justice under the *ancien régime*.

Mr. Oscar Wilde
Got extremely riled.
He ejaculated, "Blow me
If I don't write 'Salomé'."
Jean-Jacques Rousseau
N'était pas Garde du Sceau
Ni moi non plus.
Et vous?
When they asked Mr. Edison
What relation he was to his father, he said, "His son:"
A curious position
For so prominent an electrician.
(666)

J. M. Barrie
Wore a Glengarry.
First of his books comes
The "Window in Thrums."
Marco Polo
Always broke down in a Solo.
He had always from his youth
A disregard for truth.
The Rev. Stopford Brooke
The Church forsook.
He preached about an apple
In Bedford Chapel.

J. M. Barrie
Wore a Glengarry.
First of his books comes
The "Window in Thrums."

Marco Polo
Always broke down in a solo.
He had always from his youth
A disregard for truth.

The Rev. Stopford Brooke
The Church forsook.
He preached about an apple
In Bedford Chapel.

GKC

1 *A Window in Thrums* appeared in 1889, *Peter Pan* not until 1904.

3 Stopford Augustus Brooke (1832–1916), Irish writer and notable preacher, left the Church of England in 1880 (while at Bedford Chapel, Bloomsbury), unable to believe in miracles.

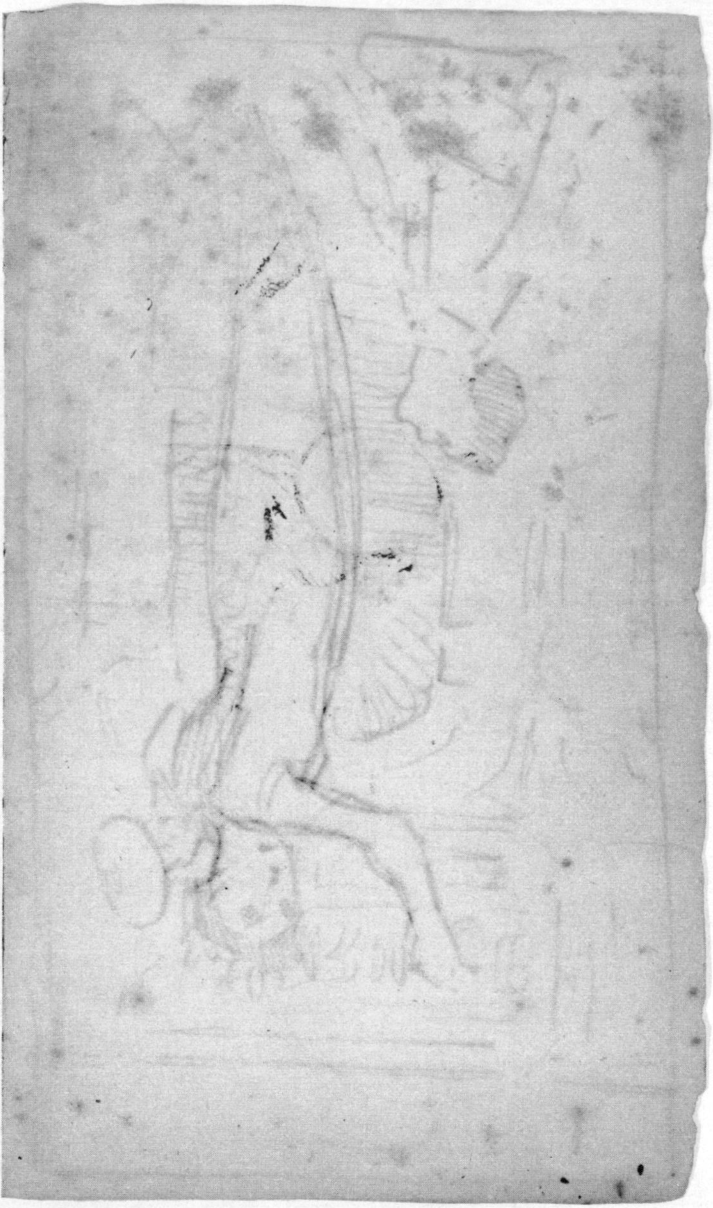

INDEX

COMPILED BY

PATRICIA UTECHIN

The principal subjects of clerihews in the notebook are given in CAPITALS.